PROLOGUE

On August 3rd 1923, in response to a question from Sean McGarry T.D., the Irish Free State Postmaster General James J. Walsh T.D. replied,

"After the transfer of the Post Office Services from the British Government on the 1st April, 1922, permits for the installation and working b of Wireless receiving apparatus were issued by the Irish Postmaster-General to experimenters and other persons who complied with the conditions laid down as regards the apparatus and aerial to be used and on payment of a fee of 10s. a year. On the outbreak of the disturbances in the country in July, 1922, these permits were withdrawn at the request of the Military Authorities and all persons in possession of wireless apparatus were required to surrender it to the Post Office for safe custody. The sale, importation or manufacture of wireless apparatus was also prohibited. This general prohibition against the use of wireless apparatus has not yet been removed. For some time past however, special permits have been given on specified conditions with the approval of the military authorities for wireless receiving demonstrations at fetes and other entertainments organised for charitable and public objects.

Applications were received from some Irish and British firms for a licence for the establishment of a Broadcasting station in the Free State. The consideration of the British applications has been deferred for the present, but in order that all persons or firms in Ireland interested in the matter might have an opportunity of having their claims considered, notifications were made in the Press inviting applications.

Numerous applications were received, and after examination and sifting three main companies were left. As it was considered that only one Broadcasting station, which should be in Dublin, was warranted if there was to be a reasonable chance of success the firms were asked to confer together with a view to uniting in a joint scheme.

The parties having failed to agree on a plan of co-operation the Postmaster-General summoned them to a Conference and laid down the general conditions on which he would be prepared to grant a licence for broadcasting. These were as follows:

1. That a Broadcasting Company should be formed with a guaranteed capital of not less than £30,000,

which would undertake to erect and operate a Broadcasting Station in Dublin.

2. That the Company should be open to any bona fide firm or person carrying on business of manufacturing wireless apparatus in the Free State on taking one or more shares in the Company. The Board of Directors should consist of seven members nominated by the constituent Companies.

3. That the licence should be for five years and to be renewable thereafter at the pleasure of the Postmaster-General. Power would be reserved to terminate the licence at any time for failure to fulfil its conditions.

4. That the importation of wireless sets or component parts of sets should be confined to the Company and its members.

5. That the Company would be at liberty to manufacture and sell wireless receiving apparatus and would receive a share of the fee to be charged by the Post Office for licences in accordance with the following scale:

Ordinary Licence Fee, £1 a year. Company's share, 12s. 6d. Private Constructor Fee, £2 a year. Company's share, 32s. 6d. Schools & Institutions Fee £1 a yr. Company's share, 12s. 6d. Hotels, Restaurants, Public Houses, &c. Fee, £5 a year. Company's share, £4 10s. Occasional Licence Fee, £1 each. Company's share, 12s. 6d. Traders' or Dealers' Fee, £1 a year. Company's share, £1. Amusement Purveyors' Fee, £1 a week. Company's share, 90 per cent.

These terms were found to be generally acceptable to the three firms referred to, but while two of them were willing to join in the formation of the proposed

Broadcasting Company they could not see their way to co-operate with the third party. The Postmaster-General met the representatives of the firms in a further Conference and endeavoured to induce them to reconsider their attitude, but without success. He explained that he could not grant a licence to a Company which sought to exclude another Company from participating in the concession, and stated that unless agreement were reached, he would have to terminate the negotiations and consider the whole question again. As agreement between the three firms has not been reached the whole matter is now being reconsidered and further applications are being invited. In the meantime, it is not possible to release wireless apparatus generally.

The Marconiphone
The Triumph of the Master Mind

2BP CALLING

In the same month as the Postmaster General was speaking to the Dail and just three months after the end of a bitter Civil War, that itself had followed on from a prolonged War of Independence, the first licensed Irish radio station took to the airwaves in Dublin. History shows that 2RN, the original RTE Radio, officially went on the air on January 1st 1926 but it was in August 1923, when station call sign 2BP began to entertain Dubliners until the newly constituted Irish Free State Government suddenly intervened and shut it down without warning or explanation.

Dublin, 15th August, 1930.

WIRELESS BROADCASTING.

THE POSTMASTER-GENERAL invites applications from Irish persons or firms who are prepared under licence from him to undertake the establishment and operation of a "Broadcasting" Station in Dublin for the supply to the public, by means of Wireless Telephony, of Concerts, Lectures, Theatrical Entertainments, Speeches, Weather Reports, etc. No application will be considered which has not been received on or before the 20th August.

Applications should be addressed to:—

THE SECRETARY,
GeneralPost Office, Dublin.

W.H.00.

On August 15th 1923 an advertisement had appeared in the Freemans Journal newspaper stating,

> 'The Postmaster General invites applications from Irish persons or firms who are prepared under license from him to undertake the establishment and operation of a 'Broadcasting' station in Dublin for the supply to the public by means of Wireless
>
> Telephony of concerts, lectures, theatrical entertainments, speeches, weather reports etc, no applications will be considered which has not been received on or before the 20th August.'

It was interesting that the Postmaster General used the phrase, 'from Irish persons' in his advertisment, perhaps designed to force Marconi out of the running for the application. Marconi had however set up an Irish subsiduary in advance of any possible application.

On the same day in the Irish Independent one of the first

advertisements of its kind appeared in the newspaper

signalling something different, something new,

WANTED—Artistes (Vocal and Instrumental) to Broadcast Solos for the Marconi Co.'s Exhibition at Dublin Horse Show. Apply Braid, c/o Pigot and Co., Ltd., 112 Grafton Street, acting for Marconi Co.

AD PLACED IN THE IRISH INDEPENDENT AUGUST 15TH 1923

The 'Braid' mentioned in the advertisement was Mr. Lennox

Braid[1] who was the sales manager at Pigott and Company in

Grafton Street.

The Irish newspapers were daily talking about 'wireless' and

speculation was mounting as to how a station would be

opened by the new Free State. Newspaper adverts by wireless

set dealers were announcing that, 'we can give immediate

delivery of the cosmos'.

---

[1] Lennox Braid died November 1944

11

The medium of wireless was gaining attention in Ireland from

unusual quarters. A year earlier many of those who tried to

advance the growing interest in radio were the clergy who

found safety behind the walls of parochial houses and monasteries.

One of those was Father John Ryan CM who taught at Blackrock College and at one time had Eamon DeValera as a pupil. On Wednesday April 5th 1922, he is credited for having organised the first radio broadcast specifically dedicated to an Irish audience. For that unique occasion, the event did not take place in Blackrock College on the southside of Dublin but northside of the city at Castleknock College. The broadcast caused quite a stir in the media and while it was an Irish audience that would be entertained the broadcast itself came from Paris.

Over a hundred students and interested amateurs filled the concert hall of the Castleknock College. The lecture began at seven o'clock and according to a journalist who was in attendance,

> 'The Reverend lecturer " tuned up" and throughout the hall we heard " dot and dash " from Clifden, Paris, Nauen (Germany), Karlsborg (Sweden), Warsaw, Moscow, and from ships at sea. A gentleman in the audience actually took down and de-coded some of the messages there and then.'

Ninety minutes later the Reverend nervously checked his watch and then he made some small adjustments to his equipment on stage, that had been supplied by the dealers Dixon and Hempenstall. The audience at Castleknock College were now so quiet you could hear a pin drop, were suddenly startled and astounded in equal measure.

> 'Suddenly there crept through the hall sweet notes of a French soprano singing " La Patrie" - A pause -

14

Now a baritone's full notes resounded in an appealing ballad. - Another pause - An orchestra playing most tunefully delighted our ears. - Another pause - Once again the soprano sang, concluding with the strains of "La Marseilles." Then a gentleman's voice was heard to say "Bon Soir mesdames, Bon Soir, messieurs.

Imagine our amazement. We had heard a concert transmitted by wireless telephony. Then came the explanation. Father Ryan, having often heard music by telephony at his station at Blackrock, conceived the daring idea of writing to General Ferrie, at the Eiffel Tower Wireless Station, Paris, to ask for the transmission of some music by telephony at 8.30 p.m. on April 5, as he would lecture on "Wireless" that evening to the Castleknock students.'[2]

---

[2] Freeman's Journal

The Paris concerts were broadcast on 2600 metres, normally aired in the afternoons as amateur listeners with experimental crystal sets listened to music concerts from Marconi's experimental station at Chelmsford, 2MT, in the evenings. Ryan believed that relaying an English broadcast might incite passions after the recent end to the War of Independence. He contacted Gustave Auguste Ferrié (19 November 1868 – 16 February 1932), who was a renown French radio pioneer and inventor and appointed a general in the French army. In 1903 Ferrie proposed setting aerials on the Eiffel Tower for long-range radiotelegraphy. Under his direction a transmitter was set up in the tower, and its effective range had increased from an initial 400 km (250 mi) to 6,000 km (3,700 mi) by 1908. He would later develop mobile transmitters for military units which would be used by the French military during the First World War. It was fortuitous that the Paris Station based at the Eiffel Tower had significantly increased its transmitter power one month earlier. Father Ryan requested of the French

General that the Paris station would organise and broadcast a special broadcast for the Irish audience at Castleknock College who were about to enter the Irish radio history books.

Writing on Ministry of War paper, Ferrie wrote to Father Ryan, which was later reprinted in the Freeman's Journal,

> 'In reply to your letter of the 21st, I have the honour to let you know that the Eiffel Tower station will transmit some musical item on Wednesday 5th April at 8.30pm GMT. I am very happy on this occasion to accede to your request.'

Then, *Paris sang to Castleknock, and Castleknock applauded enthusiastically.*

> "Ministry of War,
> "51 Cis, Boulevard Latour-Maubourg,
> "Paris, le 25-3-'22.
> "Sir—In reply to your letter of the 21st I have the honour to let you know that the Eiffel Tower station will transmit some musical items on Wednesday, 5th April, at 9.30 p.m. (summer time), i.e., 8.30 p.m. (G.M.T.).
> "I am very happy on this occasion to accede to your request.
> "Please to accept, Professor, the expression of my best wishes.
>   "FERRIE."

For decades Rule 42 of the GAA[3] rulebook forbid the playing

of what was seen as British sports, like soccer, rugby, and

cricket at GAA grounds across the island of Ireland including

its headquarters at Croke Park in Dublin. In 1923, after

several years of uncertainty due to the War of Independence

and the Civil War, the GAA urgently needed to generate

funds to pay off debts for the development of Croke Park. The

ground had become synonymous with the events of Bloody

Sunday 1920 and was a beacon of Irish nationalistic

---

[3] Gaelic Athletic Association

traditions. The anti-English sentiments had spilled over into the new Irish Free State but the GAA were desperate to fund their operations at the headquarters on Jones Road.

In June 1923, it was decided to hold a Fete or festival spanning the first two weeks in June opening on the second. Apart from sporting competitions on the field of play, markets, dancing competitions and stalls were installed on the grounds, all with one aim, to gather in as much money as they could from the paying public. The Fete was opened by Dan McCarthy TD, the president of the GAA and he suggested the optimistic plan to bring the Olympics to Croke Park. This sentiment was echoed by the then Postmaster General J.J. Walsh, both men veterans of the previous battles against the British. This launch on the steps of the main stand was the first time ever that the speeches were delivered via a loudspeaker system installed by James Kearney and his Irish and Continental Trading Company. The 'broadcasting' of the speeches to those gathered on the pitch was described by the Irish Independent as 'arousing much curiosity' and 'the first fete in Ireland where this microphone system was used'.

June 4th 1923, The Dublin Evening Telegraph

The installation of the system led to a bitter exchange between Kearney and another TD and veteran of the fight against the British going back to the Easter Rising, Sean McGarry[4]. McGarry, an electrician and businessman, seemed to be under the impression that the loudspeaker system required a licence but it didn't and he also complained that the equipment used was imported from Britain instead of being guaranteed Irish. Kearney wrote that McGarry did not know the difference between 'broadcasting' and 'listening-in'. In a letter to the Irish Independent signed by 'Fair Play', who most likely worked for McGarry, wrote,

> " As a member of the staff of an electrical
> manufacturing firm with a branch in Dublin which
> employs electrical engineers and salesmen and pays
> a large amount of money annually in wages, rates,
> and taxes in Ireland, I would like to know why
> permission for the reception of wireless broadcasting

[4] McGarry served on the Dail's Wireless Committee

is refused to legitimate manufacturers and dealers of wireless apparatus and granted to people who have no connection with the electrical industry. I see by the papers that the Postmaster-General refuses to grant any further permits, and the following day permission is again granted to certain, individuals."

It may or may not have been a coincidence that in the midst of the Fete on June 15th, the electrical supplies shop on Andrew Street owned by McGarry was broken into, ransacked and a money box taken. While the GAA leadership and membership rallied against anything English, they were not against using very specific British institutions to generate cash for the organisation, cash was King.

One of the most popular attractions at the Fete and one that required a ticket in addition to the ground entry fee, was also organised by Kearney and had received a license from the PMG Walsh. For four hours of 'wireless listening-in' to British radio stations, attendees paid an extra one schilling per head. Underneath the main stand a wireless receiving set was set up with 'perfect acoustics' and over two weeks thousands of Dubliners enjoyed the then unique experience of listening to the wireless. In 1923, there was no Irish station to listen to, so the radio was tuned into English stations relaying concerts, gramophone records and even live sports. The Belfast station had yet to go on the air and while Cardiff and Aberdeen were both audible in Dublin, the audiences at the GAA were only treated to English stations. The gramophone records heard over the ether that day were 'risqué' for many of the Catholic church faithful and didn't really sit well in the proud Irish music tradition but the younger generation flocked to the wireless room he hear the more 'decadent' modern music played by the English stations.

The Dublin Evening Telegraph reported on June 6th,

'Last night[5] a most enjoyable programme was listened to by appreciative audiences. First, we had Manchester[6], which entertained us with music and song, then we switched to Newcastle to avoid a lecture which was not of great interest. From Newcastle[7] we had some fine dance music admirably rendered. When this station announced it was closing down at 10.30, we switched onto London[8]. After some orchestral selections we got news straight from the ring about the Ratner-Todd fight[9]'.

---

[5] June 4th 1923
[6] 2ZY
[7] 5NO
[8] 2LO
[9] Roland Rodd enjoyed a points victory over Augie Ratner (USA) at Kensington, London on 4 June 1923,

While the GAA held their fierce anti-English attitude, they saw no wrong in their embracing distinctly British culture broadcast over the airwaves.

Mr. Dan McCarthy speaking into the " broadcaster " at the opening of the Croke Park Fête.   [Freeman Photo.]

In advance of the Dáil tackling radio broadcasting, in August 1923 the Marconi company, who had hoped that they would be chosen to run a commercial broadcasting service in Ireland, applied to the Postmaster General J.J. Walsh, for a temporary license to broadcast programmes for the during of the famous RDS Horse Show. The plan required a studio, transmitter, and an aerial to be erected at the Royal Marine Hotel in Dun Laoghaire and receivers set up in the RDS for visitors to 'listen-in' to this novel attraction.

The annual RDS Horse Show was a major showcase event in the capital and in 1923 it took on added significance as this was the first show held since the creation of the new Irish Free State. The show would be held from August 14th – 17th and while the sale of horses and the show-jumping events took centre stage, the Irish Art Industries Exhibition would be held alongside the main events. This was a showcase for producers and manufacturers to sell to the thousands that would attend.

Some of the stands from the 1923 RDS Exhibition

Once permission had been received, the Marconi Company

dispatched Louis Edward Wilson to the city to set up the

operation. Wilson, who described himself on census forms as

a 'publicist' married Ethel Violet Andrews on February 21st

1925 in London. Wilson had been involved in the various

temporary stations that the Marconi publicity department had

set up.

A studio with a piano forte was established on the ground

floor of the hotel, a transmitter was transported by ship to

Dun Laoghaire from the UK, where it had been successfully

used in London and Glasgow and an aerial erected in the bell

tower of the hotel. The receivers were originally placed in the

West Hall of the RDS in Ballsbridge but when test broadcasts were carried out, nearby telegraph lines were causing severe interference and the receivers were moved outdoors to the Industrial Fairs exhibition area.

(c) The RDS Archives

The Steward in charge of the 'Marconi Wireless Demonstration' on behalf of the RDS was Horace Poole, a noted scientist. When he died in January 1962, the RDS published the following obituary,

> 'Dr. Poole was noted both as a scientist and an administrator. He collaborated with the late Professor John Joly in the control and organisation of the Society's Radium Institute and, after Professor Joly's death, assumed sole responsibility for it until it was handed over to the Irish Radiological Institute in 1952. He was awarded the Society's Boyle Medal in 1936, in recognition of the value of his work in physical science'

The 2BP call sign that the Marconi company employed for the Dublin station had previously used when carrying out radio broadcast experiments. 2BP was first used in London at a Motor Show. According to Jonathan Hill in his book 'Radio Radio',

> 'In November at the Olympia Motor Show, Marconi's and Daimler carried out experiments intending to exploit the commercial possibilities of car radio. An experimental receiver was mounted adjacent to the back seat of a limousine to pick up programmes sent from a temporary Marconi transmitter (call-sign 2BP) set up in Olympia for the duration of the show'

The broadcasting station, proving its mobility, was then transported to Glasgow, where on 415m medium wave on January 23rd 1923, the next 2BP went on the air. The station continued to broadcast until February 3rd 1923. The studios were located at a Daimler garage on Hughenden Road, Kelvinside. According to Scottish radio archives,

'2BP was the call-sign of Scotland's first broadcast radio service, a temporary station established in Glasgow in January 1923 by the Marconi Company and the Daimler Motor Company. It was necessary for the purposes of promoting Daimler-Marconiphone car radios at the Scottish Motor Show of January 1923, given that the British Broadcasting Company's own station in the city, 5SC, would not be launched until March of that year. Recognising the pent-up local demand for a regular broadcasting service, 2BP's sponsors decided to extend the programme for the benefit of those who had invested in domestic receiving sets. With a regular, published programme schedule, it qualifies as Scotland's first radio station.'

GLASGOW BROADCASTING STATION.

Transmitting set showing, from left to right, the rectifier panel, the drive panel, and the main oscillator. At the extreme left, under the "Danger" notice, can be seen one of the main transformers.

Battery cabinet and battery control panel at the studio.

1923

It was a draper's assistant, born on the Upper Rathmines Road, Dublin, who would become both a pioneer in radio broadcasting in Scotland and pave the way for another giant of global communications, Ryanair, to gain a foothold in affordable air transportation into Scotland. Months before the newly formed British Broadcasting Company (as the Corporation was originally known) launched their official Glasgow radio station, 5SC, in March 1923, Frank Milligan provided the Glaswegians with their own radio station, becoming a pioneer before the arrival of the BBC.

Francis Marshall Milligan was born on July 5th 1883 at 111 Upper Rathmines Road, the eldest son of the seven children of Wicklow born accountant Andrew Mease[10] and Tipperary born Amelia Boardman. After a brief education, he began work as a drapery assistant in Rathmines but in February 1901 he joined the Imperial Yeomanry [11] of the British Army

---

[10] Ancestry.com

and found himself on the frontlines of the battlefields of the Boer War in South Africa. After being demobbed, he made his way to London and met and fell in love with Elise Adriene Barrett. Elise was better known as Elise Barone (b. London 1883 – d. Scotland 1971) and was an actress starring in silent movies such as 'Tom Cringle in Jamaica' in 1913 and 'A Flirtation at Sea' also that year. She also appeared in numerous, what became known as, cliff-hanger serials, an early form of soap opera. Her acting career ended when she married Frank in Paddington in July 1913.

The couple made their way to Glasgow, where Frank, having learned about the use of wireless in South Africa, opened a wireless sales business at 23-25 Renfrew Street in Glasgow. Milligan then found a partner to help him expand his fledgling business in George Garscadden, who ran a domestic appliance business at nearby 202 Bath Street in the city. In

---

[11] UK Military Records, Kew Gardens

October 1922, the two men gather the necessary equipment to broadcast on the fourth floor of 141 Bath Street[12]. The Milligan and Garscadden's station would be known as 5MG (also known as Milligan's Wireless Station) and broadcast on 440m medium wave. At a of the meeting of the Wireless Club held in the Scout Hall, Southbridge Street on Saturday October 14th 1922, it was revealed that a concert from Writtle[13] would be listened to,

> 'Also, a concert specially transmitted for the meeting by the direction of the demonstrator Mr. F.M. Milligan FRGS from his own station.'

The first broadcast from 5MG took place from 7pm on Tuesday October 17th 1922[14].

For their opening broadcasts the station broadcast gramophone records using a 'Algraphone'. The 'Algraphone'

---

[12] Scotland On Air
[13] 2MT
[14] The Airdrie and Coatbridge Advertiser

was made between 1922 and 1926 by Alfred Graham & Co, who were better known for their Amplion loudspeakers, for whom Milligan was the franchisee in Glasgow. Live concerts began in the cramped studios with Herbert Carruthers on piano and Garscadden's daughter Kathleen singing. Kathleen later revealed,

> 'I and my choir, in which I sang, and my organist Mr. Carruthers were invited to that little flat to come and experiment to see if we could send our voices through the air. It was really a comical set-up with cables from the kitchen to the dining room in the little flat, and a microphone like a soup-plate suspended from the ceiling. And we played and we sang night after night, but nothing happened But I'll never forget the night I was heard and my mother heard me in Sauchiehall Street, and of course that was a miracle.'[15]

---

[15] 'Carrocher in Conversation', *BBC Radio Scotland*, 3 April 1980.

The station continued to entertain ever evening from 7pm with the Glasgow Herald saying that,

'The entertainment has been of first class quality'.[16]

While Frank Milligan was creating radio history, he was also looking after a newly born daughter of his own, Madeline Primrose Milligan, born in April 1920. Primrose would go onto have her own stellar career in radio, initially as an impressionist and also on another new medium, television. According to her obituary in the Stage newspaper following her death on August 19th 1999,

"I was always in there, trying," she once told me. "Then one day I 'plunked' school to go to Glasgow and audition for a bigger contest at the Empire." That show, Brian Michie's 'Youth Takes a Bow', is part of history because of two teenagers who competed with Primrose. They were Eric

---

[16] Glasgow Herald December 1922

Bartholomew and Ernest Wiseman, remembered today as Morecambe and Wise. The girl from Prestwick (where she lived for most of her life) had savoured an early taste of showbusiness, running around her father's embryonic radio station. Those years were recalled when she featured prominently on the BBC Scottish Home Service as a leading member of the Jimmy Logan/Stanley Baxter comedy series 'It's All Yours'. Primrose joined in with all the show's gags, sketches, and catchphrases. The series still well-remembered was an early landmark in a career that embraced music hall, seaside summer shows, revue, drama productions and a tour to North America with plays from Glasgow's Tron Theatre. Primrose also worked in films in London and, in-between the performing jobs, as a fashion show compere. More recently, in her sixth and seventh decades, 'Primmie' enjoyed the fun of team camaraderie in the studio and on Loch Lomond-side location, playing Mrs Woods, a villager of fictional Glendarroch, in popular Scottish soap Take High Road. She also took cameo roles in Rab C. Nesbitt and other TV series."[17]

In early 1923 there was a buzz created into city as a second temporary station took to the airwaves when Marconi on behalf of the Daimler motor company launched a brief station 2BP to promote the sale of in car radios. On March 6th 1923, the BBC station 5SC came on the air in studios above Garscadden's shop on Bath Street and using much of the equipment that had brought 5MG to the airwaves. Kathleen followed her father's footsteps and the now experienced Kathleen Garscadden and Herbert Carruthers would join the new station, Carruthers as musical director and Kathleen as a singer and entertainer known on air as Auntie Kathleen. Lavinia Dervent writing in Dundee Courier[18] recalled,

---

[17] The Stage August 26th 1999

'The BBC under Lord Reith kept such a tight hold on the purse strings that the habit was difficult to break and employees hesitated before requisitioning even a new pencil. Yet, in spite of such restrictions, Auntie Kathleen in her day was a power in the land and will always inhabit a special niche in the annals of broadcasting, along with Uncle Mac (Derek McCulloch) who operated from London. For many years Kathleen's was the best-known voice in Scotland, eagerly listened to in cot and castle. She provided wholesome entertainment for myriads of young listeners—for old ones, too'.

Kathleen Garscadden died in Glasgow on February 20th 1991.

The Milligan's, once their station was closed and competition increased in the radio sales, moved to Prestwick where Frank was appointed the Provost of Prestwick. A Provost is the

---

[18] February 19th 1990

convenor of the local authority, the civic head and the lord-lieutenant of one of the principal cities of Scotland. In that position, after the end of the Second World War, he pushed hard for the former air base at Prestwick to adapted as an international airport. His persistence was rewarded and in his role as Provost was on hand to meet and greet famous celebrities including Princess Margaret in 1950 as she holidayed in Scotland and Queen Juliana of the Netherlands who stopped off as she made her way to the United States. Prestwick Airport[19] also made global headlines when it is one of the few places in the UK where Elvis Presley landed. Frank Milligan died on November 1st 1956[20]. According to Tim Wander's book '2MT, Writtle, The Birth of British Broadcasting' some of the radio callsigns assigned to the Marconi company included 2BN, used for general testing, 2B0 Writtle later to be changed to 2MT, 2BP was assigned to Marconi publicity broadcasts and 2BQ also used for general

---

[19] A hub for the Irish airline Ryanair
[20] The Stage trade newspaper.

testing. Their 2BP transmitter used to broadcast in Dublin was
to be found on 390m medium wave.

The Orchestra performing in the grounds of the RDS during the Horse Show
© RDS Archives

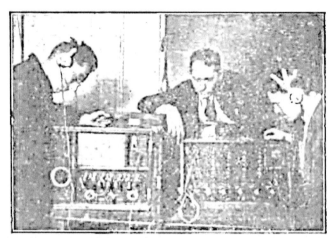

" Marconiphone " and " Amateur Wireless " technical experts testing the quality of reception. Note the power amplifier on the right. In the centre is Mr. L. E. Wilson, the " Marconiphone " publicity manager.

The Marconi company had proved their abilities to set up and exhibit the new modern technology of radio broadcasting and it was a coup that Dublin would be their next location.

The Horse Show was officially declared open on Tuesday August 14th 1923 it was time for the radio station to begin broadcasting. Just after 11a.m., a voice, 'clear and distinct' greeted listeners,

'2BP speaking.'

Once the announcer, Louis Wilson, had greeted listeners, he
introduced the first act.

'The next item on the programme will be a piano

forte solo by Miss Clarke Barry'.

Miss Victoria Clarke Barry was the daughter of a well-known
Dublin orchestra leader John Clarke Barry, who happened to
be performing on the grounds of the RDS as his daughter
mastered the new medium. Another daughter, Billie, would
go onto found the Billie Barry Acting School which was for
many decades associated with a variety of shows staged at the
Gaiety Theatre. For John Clarke Barry and his Orchestra to be
performing in the grounds of the RDS was in itself a novelty
as no live music had been allowed since 1913. An
entertainment tax, installed under British rule, had been lifted
by the then the acting Minister for Finance W.T. Cosgrave

allowing both Clarke Barry's Band and the Army band entertain visitors to the Horse Show.

 Other acts to appear included Lionel Cranfield leader of the Rathmines and Rathgar Musical Society whose lead soprano May Doyle also entertained. In April Cranfield had played Jack Power in 'The Yeoman of the Guard' opposite May Doyle as Elsie Maynard, in the Gaiety Theatre. The gramophone records that were played were provided by Pigott and Co, Dublin. According to the Irish Independent journalist who was amongst the reporters given a sneak preview of station studios in Dun Laoghaire,

> 'These demonstrations were for the purpose of
> bringing home to the Irish people the wonderful
> strides made in England in this branch of scientific
> invention and giving them an insight into the
> methods adopted by the British Government, which
> controlled broadcasting and prevented the state of

chaos which prevailed in America by reason the fact
that everybody there is allowed to transmit.

He *(Louis Wilson)* explained the powers of the
instrument being used and said thousands of people
with 30 miles of the broadcasting station could listen
in by means of a crystal machine at the cost of a few
pounds.'

While the broadcasts from Dun Laoghaire entertained during
the morning for anyone who could listen between 11am and
noon, visitors to the RDS in the afternoons were treated to the
broadcasts from the stations in Manchester and Newcastle
between 2.30pm and 5pm. While Wilson looked after the
transmissions from Dun Laoghaire, Frank Clark, also from
the Marconi headquarters in London, looked after the
reception apparatus at the RDS.

The radius of 2BP from their transmitter site in Dun

Laoghaire

Mr. John Gill,

Principal Tenor, Vicar-Choral, St. Patrick's Cathedral, Dublin, who was the first vocalist to broadcast in Ireland.

Also heard on 2BP was the principal tenor of St. Patrick's Cathedral, Mr. John Gill.

Residents of Dun Laoghaire had already enjoyed the novelty of wireless broadcasts courtesy of the Marconi company for the local fete in May 1923.

According to the advertisement for 2BP's launch, 'all communication to Mr. J.J. Kelly, 35-36 Upper Camden Street'. When Mr. James Joseph Kelly passed away in 1954, he had served the city on the City Council and was a former High Sheriff of the city. In 1916 during the Easter Rising, while running his tobacco shop on the corner of Upper

Camden Street and Adelaide Road, he was arrested by the British who had mistakenly identified him as Tom Kelly. When Captain Bowen-Colhurst, who had arrested the pacifist Francis Sheehy Skeffington, reached Kelly's shot, two journalists taking shelter inside, Thomas Dickson and Patrick McIntyre were arrested and they along with Skeffington were taken to Portobello Barracks by Bowen-Colhurst and were summarily executed. Kelly, who was not in his shop at the time discovered that the British following the arrests had used explosives to burn his business. After the arrest, he was deported to prison in England but following his case being raised in the House of Commons as a case of mistaken identity, he was released.

The 2BP broadcasts proved extremely popular not only in the RDS grounds but around the city. Listeners at Dixon and Hempenstall's shop on Suffolk Street and at Hogan's Wireless store on Henry Street gathered in large numbers and were also able to tune into the 2BP broadcasts. The novelty of hearing performances through the ether was causing quite a stir. As artists performed in front of the Royal Marine Hotel microphones, the Government of the new Irish Free State were suddenly getting cold feet after allowing a commercial company access to the Irish airwaves. This came at a time when the Dail was about to appoint a 'Wireless Committee' to discuss the merits of whether an Irish station should be State controlled or in the hands of commercial companies.

According to Louis Wilson, the Marconi engineer he said in a letter to the Irish Independent published on the 17th under the heading 'Abandoned by Order' referring to the previous day,

'Owing to a request we received from the Postmaster General we were obliged today suddenly to abandon the wireless demonstrations we were giving on behalf of the Dublin Horse Show. The request took us completely by surprise and through of course we had to accede to it, I regret that the suddenness should have resulted in any disappointment to visitors to Ballsbridge. Equally I do regret that several ladies and gentlemen who so kindly came, as arranged, to Dun Laoghaire to assist us in our efforts to demonstrate to the Irish public the possibilities of broadcasting should have been inconvenienced.

Your Dublin artistes, amateur and professional have placed us under a deep debt of gratitude. Indeed, since our arrival, we have received on all sides nothing but kindness and willingness, perhaps I should call it eagerness, of all of whom we called to assist us will be forever remembered by my colleagues and myself. It was for most of us our first experience of Irish hospitality, we shall never forget it.

It may interest your readers to know that amongst the artistes who have assisted us we have discovered several who possess ideal voices for wireless transmission and this fact it will give me great satisfaction to report to the broadcasting authorities in London. I feel that if such a programme as we gave for instance this morning could be transmitted from London, it would be enthusiastically received by our listeners.'

Wilson seemed to suggest that if the Marconi company could not gain permission to broadcast in Ireland, that Irish artists could travel across the Irish Sea and perhaps transmitters based in the UK could broadcast back into Ireland similar to how the offshore pirate ships did in the 1960's.

CLIFDEN SPORTING CARNIVAL.

On 15th, and 26th August '23.

15th August.

GRAND DRAWING OF PRIZES.

ALL DAY DANCING in Town Hall.
CONCERT IN EVENING. Palmistry. Etc.
DUBLIN and PROVINCIAL ARTISTES will contribute.
BROADCASTING and LISTENING-IN DEMONSTRATIONS on 15th and 20th by Marconi Officials. First in West, second in Ireland.

© The Connaught Tribune, August 11th 1923

The plans by the Marconi company and initially the Postmaster General seemed to indicate a wider use of broadcasting in Ireland. In advertisements in the Connaught Tribune for the Sporting Week and Fair at Clifden later that month, they advertised that 'Broadcasting and Listening-in Demonstration on 15th and 26th by Marconi Officials' would take place. It was not just listening in but also broadcasting and the advertisement said this was 'the first in the West and the Second in Ireland'. Off course the first would have been the broadcasts from the Royal Marine. The choice of Clifden would be significant for any second broadcast as the Marconi Wireless station that was used for trans-Atlantic wireless telegraphy messaging had been burned down by Irregulars in 1922 during the War of Independence with Marconi seeking significant compensation from the new Irish Free State Government. 2BP only broadcast for two days but it's power and the power of radio had demonstrated to the Government that careful consideration would have to be given as to how and who should run an Irish broadcasting service. One newspaper commentator at the time wrote,

> 'There is least one benefit of science from which we in the Saorstat are at present immune, and that is broadcasting. Broadcasting in England has added **a new terror of existence**. You cannot escape it from it anywhere, if you call into a café in the morning for a cup of coffee, you will hear it, harsh, metallic, worse than the worst gramophone, worse even than the tinniest orchestra, At lunch you cannot escape it, not at dinner. In the barber's shop or the Turkish Baths (once a haven of rest) it will grate on you.'

For hundreds of thousands of viewers, RTE's 'Dancing with The Stars' is a must watch as professional dancers, paired with celebrities attempt to impress the Judges including Lorraine Barry. Her family have had their talents showcased on the Irish broadcasting landscape for longer than you might think.

Miss Renee Flynn as she is appearing in the Prologue to "The Forbidden City," a Norma Talmadge film, showing at the Corinthian all this week.   —"Evening Herald" Photo.

In a predominately male dominated world, radio in its infancy

had two Irish female pioneers and after almost 100 years, it is time to celebrate their contribution to Irish broadcasting history. First up is Renee Flynn, a soprano that has appeared on every radio station to broadcast in Ireland up to the Second World War. Renee from Monkstown in Dublin had competed in and won several Feis Ceoil's and was proving popular across the city.

Born in Limerick in 1905, Renee and her family lived in Roscrea in County Tipperary. Her mother was a talented singer and she met Renee's father while singing in the local Church of Ireland choir. Renee appeared on stage for the first time singing nursey rhymes aged just three. At the age of fourteen she moved to Dublin where she studied to become an opera singer. In 1922, she joined the Rathmines and Rathgar Musical Society and received excellent reviews when the Society performed in the Gaiety Theatre. In 1990 she was interviewed by a family friend about her life on stage and she spoke about her role on 2BP.

'I did an enormous amount of broadcasting. I was
one of the original broadcasters, and various people,
of course, some of them were long dead, the people
then, because they were older than I, than I was, you
see. And the most extraordinary thing happened.
Nobody would know anything about this.

I know I was 18 at the time. It was the year I won the
Dennis O'Sullivan medal and I had been staying
down with my teacher and they, she and her husband
had a summer house that they used to retire to down
in Greystones. And I used to be always up and down
there with my music and I'd be working with her
because she took me on.

You wouldn't remember Lennox Braid. You know
Mary Braid, when Mary's father, and then Eileen,
her sister, of course, the two sisters, both pianists, he
was the manager of Pigott's and he used to bring me
around a lot. He was a beautiful accompanist. He

was full of music. We were living in Longford Place in Monkstown. I got a message. Actually, no phone. I can't remember how I got it. Somebody must have been sent out with it from Braid to say the horse show was on. It was Horse Show Week that the BBC[21] had come over and they had taken a over the tower building in the middle of the Royal Marine Hotel. Well, they had taken over that room and they had brought over all their, if you saw the stuff they had with them, you know, cables and things on Tri-pods, or whatever you call them, legs all over the place and things on beds. And they were getting people to sing into a telephone. And it was into the RDS and there was a little caboose and they got the people into this, but they charged them six pence or something listening to the people singing out here. That was the very first time anything in any way in

---

[21] Renee falsely remembered as the BBC rather than Marconi

that line of broadcasting was done here before we ever had a station here and it was in the initial stages in England.

Although I remember there was a very good baritone called Mikey Gallagher and he sang. And my sister, my late sister, she came along and played the accompaniments. I remembered my music was down at Greystones. I rushed out with a half-crown in my hand, charging down the slope down from Longford Place to Salthill railway station, getting myself a two penny return ticket to Greystones. Charging up from the train which went to turn to go back to town, saying to Mrs. Patty, I have to get my music. Grabbing my music, charging back, getting on the train, getting off of Dun Laoghaire and going gasping off into the hotel. I was only 18 and the way you like to. There was Chrissie Manning a quite a good little, soprano, she sang.'

Interviewer: Do you enjoy broadcast work?

'I didn't like it at first. You just do what comes your way, you know? But I got so used to it, you didn't think about it. I didn't dislike it.'[22]

RENEE FLYNN

Michael Gallagher who had also sung on the station was a baritone who won the prestigious O'Mara Cup in 1915 for singers. He would have a career on stage and on the radio

---

[22] Interview on arhive.org

until his death in 1939 in Ranelagh. A year before his death

he had performed on Radio Eireann with Renee Flynn.

M. J. GALLAGHER,
Baritone.

A FEIS WINNER.

MISS CHRISSIE MANNING,
1 Marguerite road, Glasnevin, a soprano
winner at the Father Mathew Feis.

Sandymount born Chrissie Manning was in demand for many

of The Rathmines and Rathgar Musical Society's productions

presented in Dublin.

In January 1926 Ms. Flynn appeared in 2RN's first week of

broadcasting but this was not her first visit in front on the

radio microphone. In December 1925 she had sung on the

stage of the La Scala Theatre off O'Connell Street which was

relayed to the nearby studios of 2RN and aired live as a test broadcast for the new station. 2RN officially became the Irish

Free State's station on January 1st 1926. But even her

December broadcast was not her first as she became one of

the first women to appear on Irish radio when she broadcast

on 2BP.

PRINCESS, RATHMINES.
MANSLAUGHTER,
Starring THOMAS MEIGHAN & LEATRICE JOY
Monday—MONNA VANNA.

PILLAR PICTURE HOUSE
WESLEY BARRY.
IN
THE COUNTRY KID.
MISS CRISSIE MANNING,
THE YOUNG DUBLIN SOPRANO,
WILL SING AT 8 AND 10 O'C.
Don't Miss this Great Opportunity.

Renee sang into the microphone shortly after the station had

been visited by the President of the Executive Council,

William T Cosgrave, who was originally visiting the hotel to

meet with New York Supreme Court Judge, Daniel Cohalan,

who was staying in Dublin for a couple of days. It may or

may not have been coincidence that the famous Irish tenor Count John McCormack was also visiting Dublin with his wife and did visit the grounds of the RDS before the end of Horse Show Week. Renee and her immense talent would enthral theatre goers and radio audiences alike and she was in high demand. Not content with appearing on the first two licensed stations broadcasting from Dublin 2BP and 2RN, she appeared on the other Irish station 2BE singing with the Belfast Wireless Orchestra in April 1933. Earlier in 1931, she crossed the Irish Sea to London to appear on the London Regional Service before performing and recording with the BBC Symphony orchestra in 1936. Her broadcasting career in Ireland continued as 2RN was transformed into Radio Athlone in 1933 and when Athlone was renamed Radio Eireann in 1937, one of the first singers to appear on the station was Renee Flynn accompanied by the Irish Radio Orchestra.

INTERESTS IN THE NEW DUBLIN STATION

ENGLISH REQUESTS

CHOIR AGAIN RELAYED FROM THEATRE

Interesting and practical suggestions concerning the new Dublin broadcasting station were made by officials of the Irish Agricultural Organisation Society in an interview with an " Irish Independent " representative.

Every farmer who could afford it should, they said, have a wireless set.

Songs by Miss Renee Flynn and the " Irish Independent " Male Voice Choir were again relayed from La Scala Theatre last night, the success on this occasion being even greater than that of the night before. There was a large audience.

Miss Renee Flynn, who won the contest and secured an engagement to sing at the Corinthian on Sunday next during the showing of "The Forbidden City." A great Norma Talmage film.—"Saturday Herald."

When the experimental 2BP was on air for those three days in August 1923, not only were listeners entertained by the velvet voice of Renee Flynn but also by the piano playing of Victoria Clarke Barry. Miss Clarke was the daughter of the well-known Dublin band leader, John Clarke Barry and according to the 1901 census he was living at Dargle Road, Drumcondra with his wife Annie (nee Hughes) and their three children, sons Cecil and Herbert and Victoria who was three years old at the time of the census. Clare Victoria was born on June 13th 1897, the eldest child. She passed away in the family home in Marino in October 1990. Her father struggled with his orchestra as a new style of music at the time, American jazz was beginning to become popular. According to Naiv Gallagher in her biography of Billie Barry,

> 'The family were initially comfortably off: Clarke-Barry ran three orchestras and even wrote a waltz for Britain's Queen Mother. However, he was unable to adapt his style when musical tastes switched from orchestral to jazz, and ultimately had to move his family from their large house in Drumcondra to a smaller one in Marino. Despite this reduction in status Clarke-Barry did his best to keep up appearances: he never left the house without his hat and cloak, and when travelling by train always made sure to alight from the first-class carriage even though he had travelled in third.'

John Clarke Barry   Mrs Annie Clarke Barry

In the 1920's they advertised in the newspapers that they

could be booked by contacting them at 75 Drumcondra Road.

At the age of 21 while he was a railway accountant for the

Dublin, Wicklow and Wexford Railway Company, the Blue

Hungarian Band visited the city to introduce a new variation

of the waltz. A talented pianist and an ardent amateur

musician, he decided to become a professional, and

established his famous string orchestra. Viceregal bandmaster

for 14 years, his 30-piece orchestra was so popular at hunt

balls that his services were in demand In Britain as well as in

Ireland. He composed many waltzes including, "Evening on the River", "Moonlight on Innisfallen" and " The Lady Elizabeth Boat Song" for Trinity College Rowing Club. When he passed away in 1949 his funeral was attended by the then President of Ireland Sean T. O'Kelly.

A big family man, John, and his wife Anne would go onto have eight sons and seven daughters. Victoria at times would step into replace her father as leader of the band when her father was indisposed. Later she would form her own touring band known as 'The Lady Revellers' and had a stellar career of her own. She had answered a newspaper advertisement seeking artists to appear on this new medium of radio in 1923 for the Marconi Company. As Victoria played the piano in front of the microphone at the Royal Marine Hotel, her father's band entertained the visitors to the Horse Show itself in Ballsbridge. It must have been a great sense of pride in her father as he stood at the radio set in the RDS and heard his daughter entertaining over this new medium. Victoria

featured in the band's advertising and also accompanied her

father and the band to Belfast to appear on 2BE in October

1924 after her inaugural appearance on radio on 2BP.

MISS " VIC." CLARKE-BARRY.

Somewhat of a record has been set up by
Mr. John Clarke-Barry and his Irish professional dance and concert orchestras. For the
six weeks ended February 10 engagements were

successfully fulfilled in various parts of Ireland, when over 4,000 miles of country were
traversed. His daughter, Miss " Vic " Clarke-
Barry, the well-known pianist, is a God-
daughter of the famous vaudeville violinist,
Mr. Alf. Leonard, whose brother, " Billy," is
scoring the biggest success of his career in the
" Last Waltz " with José Collins at the Gaiety,
London.

Irish Press 1931-1995, 03.10.1990, page 2

Death of Vicky Clarke-Barry

VICTORIA CLARKE-BARRY, who died in Dublin on Monday, October 1, was the eldest daughter of the late John Clarke-Barry. She started her career as a drummer in the John Clarke Barry Orchestra which was the first to broadcast in Ireland in August 1923.

The Vicky Clarke-Barry dance band became famous all over Ireland and was famous at the Great Southern Hotel and the Royal Maine Hotel, Killkee, where the band played many summer seasons. In recent years she was the pianist for the Billie-Barrie Stage School and will be affectionately remembered by pupils as their auntie Vicky.

Victoria's younger sister Billie would become the doyen of the Irish stage when in the sixties she set up an acting school to provide trained performers for the many theatre shows in Dublin and will be forever associated with the Gaiety Theatre. Billie's own daughter Lorraine followed her mother's passion into the theatre and dancing and was a perfect choice to be a judge on Dancing with the Stars when RTE purchased the rights of the BBC's Strictly Come Dancing, known outside the UK as DWTS.

Victoria Clarke Barry pictured at a family reunion

Within the National Archives there are no records either at cabinet level or within the Postmaster General's office to indicate why the decision to remove the license. While there is no definitive archival records to indicate the closure of

2BP, I believe that there are a number of possible strands of reasoning.

Following the destruction of the Clifden wireless station by Irregular forces in July 1922, while there was pressure on the Marconi company to rebuild and reopen the west of Ireland station, the Marconi company had transferred their business to stations on the West coast of Britain. It was a blow to the local economy as the station employed almost 200 people but the emerging issue was the large amount of compensation Marconi was seeking from the new Irish Free State Government.

In an attempt perhaps to placate the British broadcaster the issuing of a temporary license to broadcast for the duration of the Dublin Horse Show and then to travel to Clifden for another temporary period was seen as lessening the impact to recoup compensation, especially with the inclusion of Clifden for 2BP. In the Dail, the PMG, J.J. Walsh told the chamber,

> 'We cannot give any definite decision
> regarding Clifden by reason of the fact that the
> Marconi Company require too high a price for the
> derelict station, and thinks because it holds certain
> monopolies and patents, we will have to pay any
> price it demands.'

A secondary issue was that of the RDS itself where the listening in station was located which required a secondary license from the PMG to allow the receiver to radiate the transmissions of the British based stations in the afternoon as well as the broadcasts from Dun Laoghaire each morning. Relations between the Government and the higher echelons of the Society were strained when the new Irish Free State government commandeered the then headquarters of the RDS, Leinster House as the venue for Dail proceedings. The chief executive of the RDS, Edward Bohane wrote in his end of year look back at 1923 that he believed it could five years, ten years or never before the RDS would get back possession of Leinster House. In one letter dated July 17th 1923 from the Society's Registrar to Raymond Jeremy of the Philharmonic String Quartet he wrote

> "Owing to the continued occupation of our lecture
> theatre by the Government our series of recitals will
> be held at the Theatre Royal."

The use of the word 'occupation' is significant. There was also disquiet within some Government circles that the RDS were claiming significant compensation from the British government who had commandeered the show jumping arena for their troops and horses during the War of Independence.

It may also have been a contributing factor that a General Election, the first in the aftermath of the Civil War was called in early August with voting to take place on August 27th.

It would be over simplistic to say that the Government simply feared the power of a commercial operator having control of broadcasting in the Free State but the retraction of the license from the Marconi company would set back broadcasting in Ireland for over two further years.

1923 Timeline

January   Government lays down the law.
                 On January 18th 1923 in 'The Evening
                 Telegraph', readers with an interest in
                 radio was left in little doubt as to the
                 legalities of 'broadcasting' rather than
                 listening. It advised,

                 'The position of the Free State in
                 regard to the question of broadcasting,
                 it may be taken for granted that
                 broadly stated (1) Broadcasting of any
                 kind is not legal yet in the Irish Free
                 State. (2) That any instruments for the
                 purpose of broadcasting are illegal. (3)
                 That any attempt to bring in such
                 instruments would be frustrated, the
                 instruments of discord on-route would
                 be sequestrated.'

February	PMG J.J. Walsh said that due to the military situation, the future development of wireless broadcasting had been suspended
March	'Listening-in' licences are being issued by the Ministry for Commerce in Northern Ireland for ten shillings.
April	The formation of the Irish Broadcasting Company.
May	
18th	A public demonstration of wireless takes place at a Fete in the People's Park in Dun Laoghaire
22nd	A meeting held in Dublin Castle between PMG & businessmen interested in setting up Irish radio station
29th	A public demonstration of wireless in the Iveagh Gardens off Harcourt Street
June	
2nd	The Croke Park Fete opens with relays

of British wireless stations.

7th	The subject of the future of wireless in the Free State is raised in the Dail in a question to JJ Walsh

August

3rd	A debate in the Dail on the future of broadcasting.
13th	Advertisements appear in the Irish Independent for artistes for 2BP
14th	11 am 2 BP opens
16th	2BP closed by order of Irish Government
16th	Newspaper advertisements from the Government seeking expressions of interest in opening a radio station
September	The White Paper on broadcasting published by the PMG
19th	A second Wireless Conference is held at Dublin Castle

October   The Formation of the Radio Association
of Ireland with Kevin Street Technical College with
Professor W. J. Lyons as President

November   It is reported that three of the seven
                companies who applied to run the new
                Irish broadcasting station have
                withdrawn

December

4th   J.J. Walsh delivers a White Paper on
                the future of Broadcasting in Ireland

14th   The Wireless Committee is agreed to
                by the Dail on the foot of a Figgis
                motion

The Irish Radio Journal' published for the first time

Sources

The Marconi Archives at The Bodleian Library

The Irish Newspaper Archives

The Clarke Barry Family

RTE Archives

BBC Archives

The British Newspaper Archives

Tim Wander

Paul Kerenza & The BBCentury Podcast

The US Library of Congress

Natasha Serne at The RDS Archives, Ballsbridge

The Royal Marine Hotel, Dun Laoghaire

Nora O'Rourke at the Rathmines and Rathgar

Musical Society Archives

World Radio History

The Irish Radio Review (Held at the National Library)

The Irish Radio Journal

Printed in Great Britain
by Amazon